REAL MONSTERS

SPOTTED
HYENA

CACKLING CARNIVORE OF THE SAVANNA

PAIGE V. POLINSKY

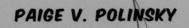

Checkerboard
Library

An Imprint of Abdo Publishing
abdopublishing.com

ABDOPUBLISHING.COM

Published by Abdo Publishing, a division of ABDO, PO Box 398166, Minneapolis, Minnesota 55439. Copyright © 2017 by Abdo Consulting Group, Inc. International copyrights reserved in all countries. No part of this book may be reproduced in any form without written permission from the publisher. Checkerboard Library™ is a trademark and logo of Abdo Publishing.

Printed in the United States of America, North Mankato, Minnesota
092016
012017

THIS BOOK CONTAINS
RECYCLED MATERIALS

Design: Christa Schneider, Mighty Media, Inc.
Production: Mighty Media, Inc.
Editor: Liz Salzmann
Cover Photo: Shutterstock Images
Interior Photos: Alamy, pp. 21, 27; Getty Images, p. 11; Mighty Media, Inc., pp. 7, 19; Shutterstock Images, pp. 4, 5, 6, 13, 15, 17, 23, 25, 29; Wikimedia Commons, 7, 9

Publisher's Cataloging-in-Publication Data

Names: Polinsky, Paige V., author.
Title: Spotted hyena : cackling carnivore of the savanna / by Paige V. Polinsky.
Other titles: Cackling carnivore of the savanna
Description: Minneapolis, MN : Abdo Publishing, 2017. | Series: Real monsters |
    Includes bibliographical references and index.
Identifiers: LCCN 2016944856 | ISBN 9781680784220 (lib. bdg.) |
    ISBN 9781680797756 (ebook)
Subjects: LCSH: Hyenas--Juvenile literature.
Classification: DDC 599.74/3--dc23
LC record available at http://lccn.loc.gov/2016944856

CONTENTS

MEET SPOTTED HYENAS

AS THEY HUNT DOWN A MEAL!!!

The sun beats down on the African plains. A herd of gazelles grazes together in the heat. But they are not alone. Three spotted hyenas wander among them. The hyenas are hungry too, and the gazelles look tasty.

Suddenly, the hyenas begin dashing and darting through the herd. The gazelles scatter. But one sickly gazelle can't move fast enough. The hyenas circle it, snapping their powerful jaws. They pull the gazelle down. Before it even hits the ground, the hyenas begin to feast.

CREATURE FEATURE

NAME: Spotted hyena

NICKNAMES: Laughing hyena, bone-crusher

CLASS: Mammalia

SIZE: 30 to 31 inches (76 to 81 cm) tall, 34 to 59 inches (86 to 150 cm) long

WEIGHT: 88 to 190 pounds (40 to 86 kg)

COLORATION: Yellow-gray with black or brown spots

LIFE SPAN: 20 to 25 years

MONSTROUS CHARACTERISTICS

> Odd sounds

> Bone-crushing jaws

> Uneven limbs

> Super speed

> Massive appetite

NORTH AMERICA

ATLANTIC OCEAN

EUROPE

ASIA

AFRICA

INDIAN OCEAN

Spotted Hyena Range

MAP KEY

SOUTHERN OCEAN

N
W • E
S

> Range: Africa, south of the Sahara Desert

> Diet: Wildebeest, zebras, Cape buffalo, gazelles, impalas, warthogs, snakes, ground birds, rabbits, porcupines, and more

FUN FACT
There are four types of hyena. They are spotted hyena, striped hyena, brown hyena, and aardwolf. The spotted hyena is the largest of the four.

7

HYENA LEGENDS

The spotted hyena is very different from any other known animal. It has a strange build. It is violent and noisy. And its appetite is monstrous. As a result, this animal has been misunderstood for centuries.

In West Africa, the spotted hyena is especially despised. Its strange appearance is frightening. And it has been known to eat farmers' livestock. But the hyena has a reputation for being more than just a pest.

The spotted hyena often appears in ancient tribal **folklore**. In these legends, its duty is rarely pleasant. It often symbolizes ugliness, stupidity, and dirtiness. In tale after tale, the hyena plays a sly, **dangerous** trickster.

Stories are very powerful. Over time, many believed that the spotted hyena was an evil monster. Some said it was controlled by witches. Others believed the hyena robbed graves. It ate dead bodies and dragged the souls away to the **underworld**. The hyena was accused of eating sleeping children and completing evil deeds for magicians.

This 1793 engraving is regarded as the first realistic illustration of the spotted hyena.

Sudanese **folklore** warns of a were-hyena that is half-man and half-hyena. This bloodthirsty beast attacks people at night. Similar warnings appear in ancient Persian writings.

Several of the myths surrounding the hyena are misunderstandings. For example, in the **Serengeti**, people would see hyenas rising from underground. Locals believed they were seeing evil spirits. Even today, their name for the spotted hyena means "spirits of the dead." But hyenas aren't ghosts. Observers were actually seeing hyenas emerge from their dens, which are dug underground.

Although hyenas are not evil spirits, they are not harmless. Each year, a small number of people are killed by spotted hyenas. Most victims are attacked while sleeping outside, unprotected. These attacks are not common. But they are enough to damage the hyena's reputation.

This bad reputation has reached the United States. After visiting Africa, former US president Theodore Roosevelt called the hyena "foul and evil." Famous US author Ernest Hemingway called it a stinking, "sad yowler." And the 1994 movie *The Lion King* presents hyenas as evil and unintelligent.

However, the hyena is just an animal following its survival instincts. Studies have shown that hyenas are quite smart. They can solve problems and adapt to new situations. From tribal legends to children's movies, the spotted hyena is deeply misunderstood.

DRAWING CONCLUSIONS

When *The Lion King* was being made, biologists asked Disney to show hyenas in a positive light. The biologists were upset with the final movie.

Kevin Richardson studies animal behavior in South Africa. Richardson works to help people understand the hyena's true nature.

FIERCE FAMILIES

The female spotted hyena is one tough mom. At about three years old, she is ready to have cubs. Her **pregnancy** lasts four months. During the last few weeks, her body produces testosterone. This **hormone** makes her cubs more **aggressive**. Higher-ranking females produce much more testosterone than lower-ranking ones. As a result, high-ranking cubs are naturally more aggressive than low-ranking cubs.

Birth is painful and **dangerous** for the spotted hyena. Firstborn cubs often **suffocate** in the birth canal. But if all goes well, the mother is left with one to four healthy cubs. The newborns have thick, dark fur. Their eyes are open and their mouths are full of sharp teeth.

FUN FACT
Hyena fathers do not help raise the young.

High-ranking hyenas usually have their cubs in a den that is shared by many. Low-ranking hyenas often find an empty den to give birth in.

The spotted hyena is born fierce. Cubs often begin fighting minutes after birth. By attacking each other, they determine who is toughest. But the fighting can go too far. Sometimes the weaker cub gets killed.

At first, the mother hyena and her cubs live alone in the birthing den. When the cubs are between two and six weeks old, they return to the clan. There, they share a den with other mothers and cubs. All of the cubs play together. But each mother cares only for her own cubs.

The mother hyena soon settles into a **routine**. In the morning, she feeds and plays with her cubs. Then, the cubs stay in the den while the mother sleeps nearby. In the afternoon, she returns to serve her cubs lunch. The hyena cubs continue to nurse over the next year. If they are high-ranking, they may receive an occasional scrap of meat.

At about three years old, the cubs are fully grown. Females stay with their birth clans. But most males join other clans to find mates.

Whether male or female, the spotted hyena leads a harsh life. It must work to find food and protect itself from predators. A hyena that is able to do so can live for more than 20 years.

MOTHER'S MILK

Spotted hyena milk is extremely high in protein. In fact, it is so filling, cubs can survive without feeding for days. This is useful when the mother needs to go on a hunting trip.

Hyena cubs begin to lose their black coats within one to two months. They grow lighter, spotted fur.

LONG LIVE THE QUEEN

Spotted hyenas live as part of a clan all their lives. There can be up to 80 members in a single clan. No other carnivores live in groups this large. Every spotted hyena clan has a **hierarchy**. And in that hierarchy, females are the rulers.

Female hyenas are larger and stronger than males. They are also more **aggressive**. A powerful female queen leads each clan. She eats first at each meal. The other hyenas follow her lead and defend her at all costs.

Male hyenas have the least power in the clan. They must respect and obey the females. When males first join a clan, they struggle to gain acceptance. Over time, a male's rank over other clan males can increase. But the highest-ranking male is still below the lowest-ranking female.

FUN FACT

A clan of hyenas is also called a cackle.

High-ranking hyena cubs quickly bond with each other.

Life is difficult for low-ranking hyenas. They are often bullied by others in their clan. During meals, they are left the very last bits of the kill. Low-ranking mothers cannot defend their cubs from higher-ranking hyenas. Much like a royal human family, spotted hyenas pass their rank on to their cubs. High-ranking cubs often tease and fight low-ranking cubs.

HUNGRY HUNTERS

The spotted hyena is not a picky eater. When it finds dying animals or old carcasses, it digs right in. Circling vultures help alert the hyena to these easy meals. Sometimes this food has already been claimed by another animal. But the bold hyena will attempt to steal it.

Because they will eat **carrion**, hyenas are known as **scavengers**. But they actually hunt more than they scavenge. The spotted hyena is one of Africa's most successful predators.

The hyena can kill prey much larger than itself. Hyenas usually work in groups to hunt larger animals. When hyenas find a herd, they walk among the animals. Then the hyenas begin to run and leap forward. The scared, confused herd scatters. Together, the hyenas circle and kill a **straggler**.

Some prey is difficult to catch. But spotted hyenas are fast and stubborn. They will chase prey for several miles. Hyenas can reach speeds up to 37 miles per hour (60 kmh).

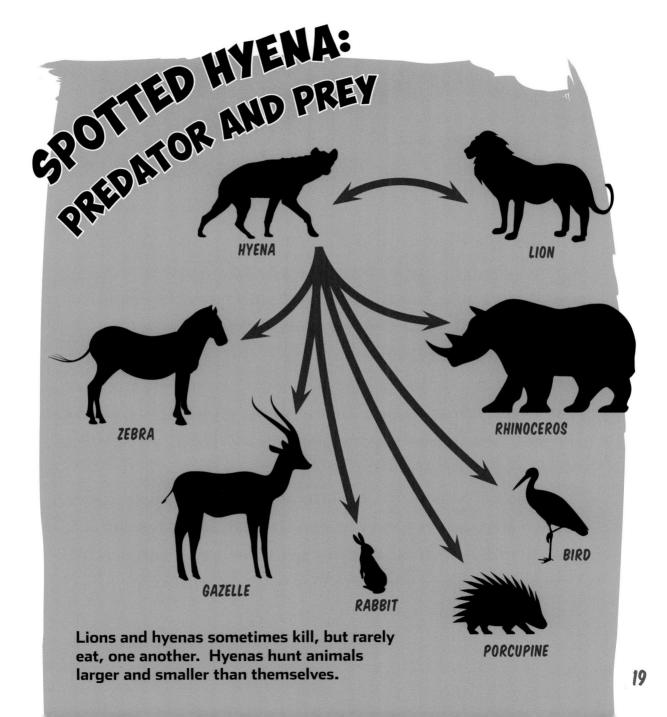

SPOTTED HYENA: PREDATOR AND PREY

HYENA

LION

ZEBRA

RHINOCEROS

GAZELLE

RABBIT

PORCUPINE

BIRD

Lions and hyenas sometimes kill, but rarely eat, one another. Hyenas hunt animals larger and smaller than themselves.

NOT SO FUNNY

The spotted hyena is the noisiest animal in Africa. Researchers have recorded more than 11 different hyena sounds. And each grunt, groan, growl, and squeal has a meaning. But the spotted hyena's most well-known noise is referred to as its laugh.

The spotted hyena is also known as the "laughing hyena." Its loud cry sounds like a strange, shrill **giggle**. But hyena laughter doesn't mean the same thing as human laughter. The hyena only laughs when it is nervous or anxious. This laughter is also a symbol of rank. Lower-ranking hyenas have a higher, more frequent laugh.

Hyenas also make whooping sounds. Each hyena has a **unique** whoop. This whoop is used to introduce, identify, and find clan members. It is also used to discuss attack plans. If a hyena finds prey or **intruders** while on patrol, it whoops for help. Its clan mates will hear the call and come running to back it up.

A hyena's whoop can be heard up to three miles (4.8 km) away.

SAVANNA SURVIVORS

The spotted hyena lives in the grasslands, woodlands, and mountains of Africa. Most especially, it roams the **savanna** south of the Sahara Desert. There, the climate is extremely hot. It is also extremely dry. During the dry season, a single **lightning** strike can set the land on fire.

But the spotted hyena is well prepared for the savanna's challenges. Its splotchy fur blends in with the tall, dry grass. Its crushing jaws and strong stomach allow it to eat anything it can catch. On a hot day, the hyena cools off under bushes or in burrows. It does most of its hunting in the cooler night air.

The wet season is much more forgiving. The spotted hyenas make use of the season's excess water. They are good swimmers and often splash around in ponds to cool off. Hyenas also use flooded areas as natural pantries. They store extra scraps of meat in the water to keep it fresh.

During the wet season, thousands of wildebeests migrate to Africa's lower plains. They provide plenty of food for hyenas.

The spotted hyena is extremely territorial. Scouts patrol their clan's borders daily. They use scent to mark the borders. Hyenas have special glands under their tails and between their toes. These glands produce thick, white paste. Scouts rub this strong-smelling paste on the grass to mark their clan's territory. Other hyenas can tell the sex and rank of the hyena that left the mark.

Spotted hyenas are not friendly neighbors. There is great tension between nearby clans, and they often war with one another. Sometimes, a hunting group ventures too close to the rival clan's border. In doing so, they risk being attacked by scouts.

When protecting its territory, the spotted hyena shows no mercy. An **intruder** often does not survive an attack. If it does, it may return to its clan with permanent damage. Hyenas have lost eyes, ears, and even lips from wandering into the wrong territory.

CITY HYENAS
Between 300 and 1,000 spotted hyenas live in Ethiopia's capital city of Addis Ababa. They eat stray dogs, dig up graveyards, and sometimes attack homeless people.

Fighting hyenas often target each other's spine, face, and ears.

ROYAL RIVALS

The spotted hyena has few enemies. Its strength, extreme fearlessness, and support of its large clan make it a powerful opponent. But the **savanna** is home to another bold, strong creature. This animal is the African lion.

Lions and hyenas fight violently over territory and food. When it comes to size and strength, the lion has the upper hand. But the spotted hyena won't back down from a challenge. It takes about three hyenas to defeat a single lioness.

Hyenas are often killed or injured in such fights. In Ethiopia, one battle between lions and hyenas lasted an entire week! Six lions and thirty hyenas died in the fight.

FUN FACT
The spotted hyena is smaller than the African lion. But an adult hyena's heart is twice the size of a lion's heart.

Despite the hyena's scavenging reputation, it is usually lions that try to steal carcasses from hyenas.

FRIGHTENING FUTURE

People are quickly replacing lions as the hyena's greatest threat. The human population keeps growing. So, hyenas must share their territory with more and more people. Because of its bad reputation, the spotted hyena is often treated very unkindly by people. It is poisoned and trapped. Sometimes it is shot on sight.

Along with being killed, the hyena is sometimes captured alive. It is then sold as an **exotic** pet. These creatures often wear **muzzles** and chains when kept as pets. They are not respected as powerful predators. Instead, they are treated as stylish objects to own.

The spotted hyena is more than a fierce, monstrous beast. It is one of Africa's **keystone** predators. It is the **savanna's** best waste collector, cleaning up any old food it can find.

There is also much we can learn from the hyena's **unique** body. The spotted hyena is able to survive diseases that usually kill other animals.

People in Harar, Ethiopia, feed spotted hyenas. It started as a way to prevent the hyenas from killing the farmers' livestock. The hyenas also help keep the city clean by eating the garbage.

This includes the fatal disease rabies. By studying the hyena, we can learn about its biology and ecosystem. We can even learn more about ourselves. And, we can save one of the world's most interesting yet most misunderstood creatures.

GLOSSARY

aggressive (uh-GREH-sihv) — displaying hostility.

carrion — dead, rotting animal flesh.

dangerous — not safe, and likely to cause harm or injury.

exotic — interesting because it is strange or different from the usual.

folklore — the stories, customs, and beliefs of the common people that are handed down from person to person.

giggle — a silly or nervous laugh.

hierarchy — arrangement according to rank or standing.

hormone — a chemical messenger that helps regulate activities in the body.

intruder — one who enters without being asked or wanted.

keystone — something necessary or very important that other things depend on.

lightning — a flash of light in the sky when electricity moves between clouds or between a cloud and the ground.

WEBSITES

To learn more about Real Monsters, visit **booklinks.abdopublishing.com**. These links are routinely monitored and updated to provide the most current information available.

muzzle — a fastening or covering over an animal's mouth to keep it from biting or eating.

pregnancy — the condition of having one or more babies growing within the body.

routine — a regular sequence of actions or way of doing things.

savanna — a grassy plain with few or no trees.

scavenge — to search through waste for something that can be used. A person or animal who does this is a scavenger.

Serengeti — an area of woodlands and grasslands in eastern Africa.

straggler — one who strays from or trails slowly behind a group.

suffocate — to die from lack of oxygen.

underworld — in mythology, the place under the ground where the spirits of dead people go.

unique (yoo-NEEK) — being the only one of its kind.

INDEX